THREE M

BOLTON TI
GENERAL E

8 12

THREE MELODRAMAS

by

ANDREW SACHS

and

RICHARD DENNIS

Edited by

MICHAEL KILGARRIFF

SAMUEL FRENCH

LONDON

NEW YORK SYDNEY TORONTO HOLLYWOOD

These plays are fully protected under the copyright laws of the British Commonwealth of Nations, the United States of America, and all countries of the Berne and Universal Copyright Conventions.

All rights are strictly reserved.

It is an infringement of the copyright to give any public performance or reading of these plays either in their entirety or in the form of excerpts without the prior consent of the copyright owners. No part of this publication may be transmitted, stored in a retrieval system, or reproduced in any form or by any means, electronic, mechanical, photocopying, manuscript, typescript, recording, or otherwise, without the prior permission of the Copyright owners.

SAMUEL FRENCH LTD, 26 SOUTHAMPTON STREET, STRAND, LONDON WC2, or their authorized agents, issue licences to amateurs to give performances of these plays on payment of a fee. **The fee must be paid, and the licence obtained, before a performance is given.**

Licences are issued subject to the understanding that it shall be made clear in all advertising matter that the audience will witness an amateur performance; and that the names of the authors of plays shall be included on all announcements and on all programmes.

The royalty fee indicated below is subject to contract and subject to variation at the sole discretion of Samuel French Ltd.

> Basic fee for each and every
> performance by amateurs
> of each of these plays   50p
> in the British Isles

In theatres or halls seating 600 or more the fee will be subject to negotiation.

In territories overseas the fee quoted above may not apply. Application must be made to our local authorized agents, or if there is no such agent, to Samuel French Ltd, London.

ISBN 0 573 00018 2

PRINTED IN GREAT BRITAIN

This impression printed by photo lithography from the original printing by W & J Mackay Limited, Chatham

CONTENTS

PREFACE

I am professionally involved in the presentation of Old Time Music Hall programmes, and became aware some years ago of the dearth of short melodrama sketches suitable for inclusion in this very popular type of show. Andrew Sachs was therefore commissioned to write *The Drunkard's Dilemma* and *The Wages Of Sin*, and my partner, Richard Dennis, came up with his version of *Maria Marten*.

I have produced all three pieces in my own shows countless times all over the world, and can assure the reader that they well and truly work.

They each have the benefits of small casts, simple staging requirements, a minimum of easily obtainable props., lots of chances for audience participation, and above all, plenty of laughs.

MICHAEL KILGARRIFF

NOTES TO THE PRODUCER

These three pieces should be played out front.

I start with this rather dogmatic statement since it is far and away the most important stylistic requirement of melodrama, and it is also the hardest for actors to acquire.

Theatrical dialogue is generally played as a conversation between the actor and another: in melodrama it should be considered perhaps as a conversation between the actor and his audience. Watch any comedy double act—Morcambe and Wise, or Mike and Bernie Winters—and you will see what I am driving at. These comics don't really talk to one another. Rather do they hand out information which is calculated to arrive at a humorous conclusion. Melodramatic conclusions were specifically designed to be strongly emotional; that is what the authors and actors were selling, and that is what they achieved.

This technique is not easily learnt, but much of the period style and flavour will be lost if the director does not bully his cast into following the "out-front" precept.

The naturalistic style of acting which emerged in the late nineteenth century was an important contributory factor in the decline of melodramas; obviously therefore we must not attempt to perform them as we would the latest Osborne or Beckett. The characters are admittedly cardboard but their emotions are real enough, albeit presented in the broadest terms and artificially forced by the hot-house plots.

But what opportunities those old plays gave to act! They were an actor's dream, allowing for full-range displays of personality and passion, unencumbered by subtleties of characterization or directors' quirks. The actor was king; he strode his stage with mighty strides, exuding a distillation of the finest virtue, the noblest sentiments—or the basest villainy, as the case may be—secure in the power of his technique and imagination to hold his audience rapt.

What a chance for a pretty *ingénue* to display her daintiness and femininity; what a chance for a leading man to portray courage and resolution. Polish, grace, "good address", a resonant speaking voice—these were just as much part of an actor's equipment as fire and guts. And he was expected to sing, dance and tumble as well!

Pick as attractive a cast as you can. Let your heroine be ravishingly pretty and your hero a fine upstanding figure of a man. Dress them gaily and light them brightly—have a couple of follow-spots if the budget can afford it.

As with any other enterprise, melodrama can be well or badly undertaken, so let us not sell it short. Ludicrous as these three short plays are, I have seen time and time again how strong emotional playing has engendered a remarkably sympathetic response which even almost constant laughter has not entirely dissipated.

However, we are concerned here with *cod* melodrama, and are principally looking for laughs, so I will stop generalizing and get down to specifics. By a curious coincidence, both my authors have appeared in various Brian Rix farces, and at the time of writing (November 1969) I myself am appearing in *She's Done It Again* for Mr Rix at the Garrick Theatre. Also the authors and I have appeared ourselves many times in all three pieces, so you have here not only three very good scripts, but a bonus of accumulated gags and business from many productions.

The playing of cod melodrama should be approached with the same attitude as the playing of farce: absolute and complete sincerity at all times, speed, and clarity.

Sincerity is obviously of paramount importance. If your audience becomes aware for an instant that the cast is conscious of the absurdities of the situations and plot, then the whole exercise becomes sterile. An audience must be allowed to make its own conclusions, and larking about on stage—whilst inevitably raising a few guffaws—will only bring pain and embarrassment to the informed spectator. The dialogue must be played for all it is worth, and I assure you that the laughs will come.

Pace perhaps speaks for itself, but it does not mean that speeches should be rushed. Your actors must elocute rather deliberately, with perhaps undue (to our modern ears) stress on individual syllables—but this must not be overdone, or it can become very tedious. Picking up cues cleanly is an attribute all too often lacking in amateur performances, but your actors should not be afraid to wait for laughs. If a laugh is inadvertently spoken through, the actor concerned must simply pause and say the line again.

Clarity means ensuring that the plot is plainly delivered, and that the audience's attention is focused on one thing at a time. Gags occurring on opposite sides of the stage must obviously not occur simultaneously, and attention must be directed at all times to where it is needed. I have endeavoured to obviate any errors of this kind in my stage directions.

The reader will notice that two of the pieces commence the same way, that is with introductory rhyming couplets for each member of the cast. Their value lies, I have found, in encouraging the audience to participate vigorously from the outset.

I would advise a long skirt and a cloak to be made available at early rehearsals since movement in these—especially when falling to the floor and rising—needs practice. An old blanket to protect clothing will be appreciated by your players.

At the conclusion of the play, the chairman, having delivered whichever gag he wants to use (one is included with each piece) should also give details of the cast. This is something else that will be appreciated by your cast.

None of these interludes should be placed in the first half of the programme. *Maria Marten* should come no sooner than half-way through the second act if there are two intervals, or towards the beginning of the second act if there is only one. It should be preceded and followed by musical items—the latter ideally a non-comedy chorus song, e.g. "Are We To Part Like This, Bill?"

The Drunkard's Dilemma can close the second act or open the third if there are two intervals, or open the second if there is only one. It should also be preceded and followed by non-comedy musical items—a suggestion for the latter being "Joshua".

The Wages Of Sin is, I have found, best placed at the very end of a programme, to be preceded by a non-comedy up-beat chorus song (say, "Mollie O'Morgan") and followed immediately by your Grand "Knees-Up" Finale.

And finally, may I repeat once again; these pieces should be played out front.

Maria Marten by Richard Dennis

Playing time 8 minutes approx.

This is the shortest and simplest of the three sketches, but it is very strong and effective. I have seen the author play William Corder more times than I can remember with a variety of Marias and Stage-Managers, and have never known it fail.

The Squire should be played on two levels: as the villain of the piece and as the actor playing the villain. He must obviously be a good actor who is constantly frustrated by his leading-lady and by a blundering stage-hand. But his sincerity must never waver, rather should his fury at the various mishaps be grafted on to the villainy of the character he is playing. His final speech must be played for real. There are no jokes there, nor are there intended to be. At last the Squire has the stage to himself and is able to give his all without interruptions, but to his chagrin the Stage-Manager still manages to hog the final bows.

He should always pronounce the word "my" as "me", and his movements must be very stylized—he moves from pose to pose, from attitude to attitude.

Maria is all things nice: her movements are balletic, and she is oblivious of the way she wrecks the Squire's efforts at high drama. She can have a country accent or not, at the producer's discretion

The Stage-Manager is very nervous at first, but as his confidence grows he is seen to become heavily stage-struck. The audience will quickly get the joke, and he will be cheered mightily at the curtain. He can also hand out and receive back the shovel, and be responsible for the off-stage gunshot.

Music should be virtually constant, as in the silent cinema. There are one or two places where silence will underline the drama, for instance where Corder says "Then you die!" and attempts to fire the gun. The music should cease here until Maria is actually shot. Nor is music necessary for the Stage-Manager's entrances.

If your audience is a little slow on the uptake, the shouts of "Upside down!" can be judiciously helped along by the usherettes or members of the orchestra.

Practically every line can be said out front. The general rule is that the speaker looks at the audience and the listener looks at the speaker; this instruction can be ignored where there is a sequence of short lines or your actors will make themselves dizzy.

At the conclusion the chairman can say: "Not a dry seat in the house . . .?"

The Drunkard's Dilemma by Andrew Sachs

Playing time 12 minutes approx.

As indicated on the cast list, the villain can be played by the chairman—in fact the part was written this way specifically at my request. There is time for the chairman to alter his make-up in the wings before his entrance, and to restore it after his exit. He should not take part in the calls but should emerge after the black-out to lead the applause. Then after the cast has left the stage he can say: "I thought the chap who played the landlord was rather good, didn't you . . .?"

The word "tenpence" should always be pronounced "ten-*pence*".

The hero and the villain must again play with very stylized movements. Every gesture and pose must be neat, precise and "considered". They must, in a word, attitudinize. Out-fronting is important as always—the laugh on the landlord's line "Well—gel?" will be lost otherwise, also the laughs on "I love you—will you marry me?" "Yes!" depend on the hero and heroine *not* looking at one another.

Uncle is a much more difficult role than would appear. He must be desperate in his first scene and very drunk in his second. These two moods must not be confused. Nor must his drunkenness be allowed to go over the top. Remember you are presenting a short play and not a variety sketch. I have seen a first-class actor, during a three-week run, actually *reduce* his laughs by over-exaggeration of the drunkenness. He was hilarious to start with, became quite hysterically funny and then overstepped the bounds of credibility, losing sympathy and laughs.

Again music should be virtually continuous. It is a good idea to give a script to your pianist at rehearsals so that he can follow the dialogue and action closely. Obviously the landlord's entrance needs a strong minor chord in the bass, just as "What's this? She's fainted!" needs silence, followed by a mysterioso chord after "Now's me chance!"

The concluding song is in 6/8 time and the dance should be very simple—remember Uncle is still rather drunk.

The Wages of Sin by Andrew Sachs

Running time 23 minutes approx.

This is the most difficult of the three and features a bravura double role for a leading lady. She is not an *ingénue*, but a most glamorous and ripely attractive lady of around thirty years of age. Mr Brown can be played by the chairman; as in *The Drunkard's Dilemma* he need not take part in the final bows, but can come on to lead the applause. After the cast had left he can use the same gag, i.e. "I thought the chap who played Mr Brown was rather good" or "There's nothing like a good play, and I'm sure you all agree that *that* was nothing like a good play . . ."

This is also the most sophisticated playlet in this book and ideally requires an audience *au fait* with the Music Hall and Melodrama tradition. The business in brackets may look complex but generally speaking is not so. It is just that the reduction of even simple sight gags to words has run me into more lineage than I would have wished. But careful and imaginative reading will, I trust, lift the production off the page.

There is no especial significance in the gradual denuding of the table-legs. It simply provides a very good opening laugh, and is a running-gag which the audience looks forward to.

May I stress yet again the necessity of playing out front? For instance on Lady Priscilla's first entrance, Lord Fortune-Mint must say "Priscilla, my darling!" out front and *then* look to the upstage entrance. Then again, Mr Brown must say "Your last moment has come, sir!" out front, flourish his gun so that all may see, and only then should he turn to Lord Fortune-Mint.

Pace and clarity are particularly important, since there is a good deal of fairly complicated plot to be explained. Get from laugh to laugh as quickly as possible.

` A good deal depends on your casting. In fact this whole piece is far less "actor-proof" than the previous two, demanding as it does experienced and high quality players.

Lord Fortune-Mint has more laughs than may be apparent on first reading: but they largely depend on the actor playing him. He must not appear too stupid as he must be a suitable husband for the bewitching Lady Priscilla and must present a convincing aristocrat. He should be very public-school and stiff upper-lip; in fact he is basically a thoroughly good type apart from that unfortunate weakness for bare table-legs. Considerable subtlety can be exercised on the role—perhaps more so than on any other in this book.

Mr Brown can be played as the traditional villain. He is not in fact a villain, but this reading makes him all the more dangerous and contrasts well with Lord Fortune-Mint.

Jasper, like Uncle in *The Drunkard's Dilemma*, can easily be overplayed. He must be very palsied but not distractingly so. I once had a Jasper who was so overwhelmingly decrepit that the audience was unable to attend to anyone else on the stage and a good deal of the plot and comedy subsequently went by the board. This is not the only difficulty of the part. He must make a convincing old man with the minimum of make-up, since after he unmasks himself he must also appear a convincing rogue. As with Lord Fortune-Mint he should be a suitable partner for Lady Priscilla, so I would advise you to cast an experienced comedy actor in his thirties or early forties.

The whole piece depends of course to a great extent on your Lady Priscilla/Mrs Brown. The part calls for an actress of more than average physical attractiveness and with a very strong personality. The two roles must be well contrasted: Lady Priscilla to be demure and rather pedantically elocuted, Mrs Brown to be the archtypal Scarlet Woman.

It is advisable for the props for this piece to be available at rehearsals as early as possible, and I would also recommend that someone be deputed to assist Lady Priscilla with her changes in the wings.

Watch the positioning of Lord Fortune-Mint and Jasper when they are dead, since as much room as possible must be left for Lady Priscilla's final speech and death.

Again music should be used extensively throughout, with

silence perhaps from Lord Fortune-Mint's first entrance until Lady Priscilla's first entrance, and also when Lord Fortune-Mint's gun fails to fire.

*　　　*　　　*

Complete piano scores for these sketches are available from Samuel French Ltd at 25p, 5s per copy.

MARIA MARTEN
OR
MURDER IN THE RED BARN

CHARACTERS

Maria Marten   A poor village girl

Squire William Corder   A villain

The Stage-Manager (non-speaking)

MARIA MARTEN
OR
MURDER IN THE RED BARN

Chairman Ladies and gentlemen, it is, as you well know, the
tradition of this house to present only the very finest artistes;
it gives me therefore the greatest pleasure to be able to announce
that our stage is now to be graced by the presence of two of
England's leading Thespians—and when I say England's
leading Thespians I mean of course the world's leading
Thespians—Sir Herbert and Lady Beerbohm Bush! These
distinguished luminaries of the theatrical profession have
graciously consented tonight to give us two scenes from that
celebrated spine-chiller: *Maria Marten,* or *Murder In The
Red Barn.*

Loud chords from the orchestra

(*Testily*) Not yet—not yet.
>Our heroine will first appear;
>Her name's Maria—so give her a cheer!

Maria enters R, *curtseys to the audience, wafts a gracious kiss to
the Chairman, and departs* L

>Here's William Corder, the wicked squire;
>Please hiss and boo this villain dire!

Corder sweeps on L, *with a big smile over his evil features. His
confident entrance is spoiled by the boos and hisses which greet
him: his smile vanishes and he responds by hissing back at the
audience. He wraps his coat round him in a defiant gesture and
exits* R, *scowling*

I will now call upon our stage-manager to set the scene.

The Tabs open

> *The Stage-manager enters* R, *carrying a card bearing the words "Maria's Kitchen". He is very nervous and shakes visibly. However, under the Chairman's encouragement—who invites the audience to applaud him—he bucks up and displays his card all around with growing enthusiasm. Indeed, it quickly becomes apparent that he is loth to leave the stage, and the Chairman has tactfully to wave him off*

Yes, thank you—yes, very good. Thank you so much . . .

> *The Stage-Manager exits* R

So now, the scene is set and the artistes are waiting in the wings. Ladies and Gentlemen, *Maria Marten*, or *Murder In The Red Barn*. (*Aside to the orchestra*) Now! (*He sits*)

Crashing chords from the orchestra, changing to sweet heroine theme ("O Star of Eve" from "Tannhauser") as—

> *Maria enters* L

Maria (*in despair*) Oh! Oh! Oooh!
A Voice (*either off-stage or from out front*) Oh—get on with it!
Maria (*recovering swiftly*) Oh, that I Maria Marten, a poor village gel, was wronged by the Squire William Corder. And did not the child of our union die of some strange illness? (*Happily*) But he shall marry me. I hold his promise here. (*She reaches into her bodice, realizes the note is not there. She turns her back on the audience and removes it from the top of her stocking*) I hold his promise here. Oh, but once I was an innocent maiden —now what am I? (*She weeps*)
Voice I could tell you!
Maria But hark—I hear his footsteps. (*She puts her hand to her* L *ear. Silence*) But hark—I hear his footsteps.

> *Corder enters* R

Corder (*as he enters*) Ha ha!

Lights flash, the music plays crashing minor chords, and the following-spot changes momentarily to green. Hisses from the audience are returned by Corder before he addresses Maria

(*To Maria, taking her hand; evilly*) Dearest Maria!

Maria Oh William, you have come at last!

Corder On receiving your note I came to you at once!

Maria (*breaking from him a little*) When are you going to keep the promise you made to me?

Corder I come to tell you that the death of my father removes the only obstacle to our union.

Maria I shall tell my parents at once.

She crosses him, but he catches her by her left arm

Corder One moment, Maria, you know the aversion me mother has to your family. Therefore I wish the marriage to be performed—in *London*!

Music: "Do not trust him, gentle maiden!"

Maria In London! Why there?

Corder Business requires me to leave at once. Therefore I wish you to meet me tonight—in the *Old Red Barn*!

Thunderous chords. Lights flash on and off

Maria No, no! Anything but the Old Red Barn!

Corder (*leering and twirling his moustache*) Anything?

Maria (*submitting to her fate*) The Old Red Barn . . .

Corder (*stroking her hand*) Do not worry, Maria, for from the Barn we shall start on our road to love and happiness.

Music reprises: "Do not trust him"

Maria Very well, I consent, and shall meet you tonight at the Old Red Barn!

Maria exits R, *smiling bravely*

The music immediately crashes into a minor chord

Corder (*laughing triumphantly*) Ha—ha!

Maria returns momentarily to blow him a kiss

Corder recovers quickly and by rapid facial gymnastics manages to give her a twisted smile

   Maria exits

(*Returning to his normal scowling self*) She consents! Curse the gel! She binds me down—me mad gambling debts have left me penniless. Only a rich marriage can save me now. Maria, when you consented to meet me in the Old Red Barn, you sealed your doom!

Music fortissimo—perhaps the opening of Beethoven's Sonata Pathetique. Lights flash

   Corder, with a flourish of his cloak, strides to exit R, *The Stage-Manager enters and there is a collision. Corder is furious at having his grand exit ruined, and slides off ignominiously in high dudgeon*

The Stage-Manager, quite confident this time, has another sign to display. This one reads "The Old Red Barn", and though it is shown round with the greatest of aplomb, it is unfortunately upside down. Shouts of "Upside down!" from the audience and the wings only serve to confuse him. He turns upstage and checks his fly-buttons, at which the Chairman gently indicates the cause of the trouble. The Stage-Manager is in no way put out; he simply turns the sign right way up and shows it round as before. Again the Chairman has to get him off stage tactfully by applauding and encouraging the audience to do the same

   At last the Stage-Manager exits R

The lights lower and the music recommences, very sinister and foreboding; again perhaps the Beethoven could be played

   Corder enters, stops and looks round to see if the coast is clear. To make sure, he strides round the stage in a big circle, and as he passes the R *entrance a hand comes out holding a shovel. Without looking at it or breaking step, Corder takes it and continues to* C. *He mimes digging*

On the first thrust of Corder's shovel there is a chord of music, then another as he throws the earth over his shoulder. This is repeated once, then Corder moves to the R entrance, but the chords are played a third time. Corder looks at the orchestra with hatred and mouths "Fool!" At the R entrance a hand comes out and takes the shovel

Corder All is completed! I await now my victim—will she come? Oh yes, a woman will do anything for the man she loves. Hark! I hear her footsteps now tripping across the fields.

Off R are heard ponderous, thudding footsteps

She has a song on her lips.

We hear Maria screeching "Nellie Dean"

Little does she know that death is so **near**! (*He goes up L and draws his cloak up over his face*)

The lights come up to full, and Maria's theme music is heard

Maria enters R

Maria William! William! (*Moving down C*) Not here? (*She backs upstage to where Corder is concealed*)

As Maria nears him, Corder lifts the cloak as if about to smother her. This usually gets a good response from the audience of "Look out!" and "Behind you!" At the last moment Maria moves RC, and Corder almost overbalances

Oh, how frightening it is here alone! I will leave this place at once . . .

Corder (*revealing himself*) Stay, Maria! (*He moves to her*)

Maria Oh William, how glad I am to see you. Let us leave this horrible place at once. (*She moves to exit R*)

Corder (*grabbing her L wrist*) One moment—did anyone see you cross the fields?

Maria (*wondering*) No one.

Corder (*chuckling*) That's good. Maria, do you remember a few days ago threatening to betray me about our child to Constable Ayers?

Maria (*with a light laugh*) Oh William—(*She sweeps her L hand across expansively, and inadvertently catches Corder in the stomach*)

Corder folds

—a foolish jest! (*Another gesture catches his top hat and rams it over his ears as he rises*)

Maria is oblivious, but Corder is furious

Let us leave this place

Corder (*straightening his hat*) No, no! Do you think my life is to be held at the bidding of a silly gel? No—look what I have made here! (*He indicates where he has been digging*)

Maria What is it?

Corder (*very big*) A grave!

A chord of music

I mean to kill you and bury your body here.

Maria Oh, no!

Corder You are a clog on me actions, a chain—(*He mimes pulling a chain*)—that stops me reaching ambitious heights. You are to die—tonight!

Maria (*weeping at his feet*) No, not by your hand, the hand that loved me. Oh, spare me! Spare me!

Corder 'Tis useless! Me mind's resolved. You die tonight!

Maria (*rising*) Wretch, since neither pity nor love will save me, Heaven will surely nerve my arm to battle for my life!

Chase music. Corder and Maria struggle, their hands interlocked on a stylized manner

Corder Foolish gel! Desist! (*He throws her from him* L)

Maria Never whiles I live! (*She moves in to renew the fight*)

Corder Then you die! (*He throws her* L *again and takes out a gun*)

The music stops. Corder pulls the trigger. There is no sound

Then you die! (*He pulls the trigger again, and again there is no sound*)

Corder turns to go off R *to see what has happened to the gunshot; he takes only two steps when the shot fires off-stage. Maria, clasps her bosom and staggers across* RC. *Corder turns on his heels and runs to catch her, misses, turns again in time to catch her and lay her gently on the stage. The lights begin to lower and the music plays sadly. ("Hearts and Flowers" is the usual choice here, but the slow movement from Beethoven's Sonata Pathetique may be preferred. It is especially effective if a violinist is available*)

Maria William, I am dying—your cruel hand has stilled the heart that loved you. Death claims me—but with my last breath I die blessing and forgiving thee. (*Her head droops*)

Corder gently lays her flat. The music stops. Corder rises, takes one step, and raises a hand and opens his mouth to speak, when Maria revives. (Ideally she should speak as Corder's foot is actually in the air)

I die! (*She drops again*)

Corder looks at her, then tries again. Again she revives

I die! (*She drops*)

Corder tries a third time, and stops himself to look at her. She does not move

Corder (*angry, but controlling himself for his final big speech*) Blessings and forgiveness for me, her murderer? (*He looks at her face*) Oh Maria, do not look so tenderly upon me. Let fire burn from your lips and curse me.

Oh, may my crime for ever stand accursed,
The last of murders as it is—the worst!

Corder exits in a swirl of cloak. The CURTAIN *falls, or there is a Black-out, to crashing minor chords.*

The music changes to "The Soldiers' March" from "Carmen" as the CURTAIN *rises and the lights come up to full. The Stage-Manager enters and helps Maria to her feet and the two of them graciously take bows. Corder comes on and pushes the Stage-Manager out of the way. The Stage-Manager goes to the other side of Maria and continues taking bows as though he had just given the finest Lear of the century.*

CURTAIN

Note: If there is no Curtain and the actors have to walk off in sight of the audience, Corder should try to be the last one off stage, but somehow the Stage-Manager takes the last call, waving and blowing kisses to his public.

THE DRUNKARD'S DILEMMA
OR
HER HONOUR FOR TENPENCE

CHARACTERS

Uncle	A gin-sodden wreck, but basically good: in his forties
Georgina	Ingenue, all things nice
The Landlord	The villain: can be doubled by the Chairman
A Man	Upright hero who turns out to be Roger, Georgina's cousin

THE DRUNKARD'S DILEMMA
OR
HER HONOUR FOR TENPENCE

APPLAUSE

The Chairman And now, Ladies and Gentlemen, we come as advertised in your programmes to our powerful and gripping dramatic interlude entitled *The Drunkard's Dilemma*, or *Her Honour for Tenpence.*

The tabs open on to a bare stage

Allow me, if you will, to set the scene.

He walks to R or L entrance and holds out his hand. A hand is thrust out from the wings holding a coat-and-hat rack which he places up C. (If possible, a single flat can also be placed upstage painted to represent a stylized poor living-room interior)

The setting is the humble but scrupulously neat and tidy living-room of a working girl and her uncle. I might mention that the elaborate scenery was purchased by a resourceful management from a sale of effects of the late Dowager Marchioness of Budleigh Salterton, who will be so greatly missed by all ranks of the Twenty-fourth Lancers—gad, she was game! Here now, to play out the piece in all its torrid torment and tempestuous tumescence—whatever that may mean—are the Billericay (or local) Barnstormers!

laugh

The Chairman sits (or exits, if he is to play the villain). Dramatic music

Uncle enters L. He is wild-eyed, fraught and desperate

Uncle Drink! I must have drink to still my aching conscience! (*He clutches at hope, putting his cap on the stand*) Somewhere in this room my ward, Georgina, keeps money in a tin for the rent that's due today. I'll have it. What's rent to a thirsty man? (*He rushes around the stage*) The money—where is it? The rent tin—must have money . . .

On the Chairman's table is a tin clearly labelled RENT, *with a flip-top lid. During his peregrinations Uncle lifts up the tin and looks under it. He puts it down with a crash and a rattle of the coins inside: he takes a couple of steps away and then realizes*

Ah! (*Returning to the tin and opening it*) Here it is. (*He puts his hand inside*)

Music plays "Home Sweet Home"

Georgina enters R

Georgina (*as she enters, singing*) "There's no place like . . ." (*She sees Uncle. Putting her shawl on the stand*) What are you doing?

Uncle faces her with his hands behind his back. One hand is caught in the tin and he is trying to get it out

Uncle Caught! Nothing, Georgina, my love. Just waiting for— (*he heaves*)—you! (*He is free. He puts the tin back on the table and moves a pace or two to* C)

Georgina Dear Uncle, I've worked five extra hours in the match factory today to earn the tenpence we need to make up the rent. (*She goes to the Chairman's table*) Now we have enough—and just in time. Isn't it wonderful?

Uncle (*catching her hand as she passes and dropping to his knees*) Oh Georgina, forgive me!

Georgina But why, Uncle?

Uncle (*about to give the game away, but the hand which he is grasping gives him an idea*) Er—for allowing you to roughen your innocent hands on menial work.

Georgina Tush, Uncle. It's only until you find employment worthy of your talents.

Uncle (*brokenly*) Bless you, my child.

Georgina (*doing a double-take over her shoulder*) But what's this—the rent tin open on the table?

Uncle (*grovelling*) The shame of it!

Georgina (*putting the tenpence in the tin and moving* C) You were counting it for me, Uncle. How kind of you.

Uncle (*aside*) The angel. (*Shuffling to her on his knees*) Yes, my dear, and I was wondering . . .

Georgina Yes?

Uncle (*rising*) I was wondering—if—(*He is so ashamed*)—if—(*looking away, but holding his* L *hand bent as though soliciting a tip*)—if there was a copper to spare . . .

Georgina Oh, Uncle, I'm so sorry, but we've only just enough for the rent with my extra tenpence.

Uncle (*aside; very big*) Curse her! Why does she keep harping on tenpence? It rings around me besotted brain. Tenpence! The price of a bottle of gin. (*To Georgina*) Me child, I will be frank with you. (*Clutching his throat*) I'm very—(*Hoarsely*)—thirsty . . .

Georgina Of course, Uncle. You're wanting your tea . . . (*She turns to exit* L)

Uncle (*grabbing her* R *wrist*) No, no! (*Tightly*) Angel! (*Controlling himself*) You misunderstand me. Me thirst cannot be quenched by tea.

Georgina You mean—(*She takes a step away*)—oh no!—alcoholic liquor?

The following six lines are spoken at great speed

Uncle Only a drop!

Georgina Oh, Uncle!

Uncle Georgina, I'm desperate!

Georgina But you promised!

Uncle Just this once!

Georgina But why?

Uncle (*breaking the pace with a great sob*) You know the reason . . .

Georgina (*sympathetically*) Your son?

Uncle (*wildly*) Yes! (*Tragically*) My son! My darling son. (*Taking the stage* C *for his big speech*) I was desperate enough fifteen years ago when my angelic wife died. But then, on our way back from the funeral, I stopped to wipe my tear-filled eyes, and in that moment Roger, my little son, let go my hand and wandered round the corner of a busy street—and was lost.

Georgina Poor . . .

Uncle (*furious because she has come in too soon; with a glare at her*) Lost! (*Recovering himself*) I searched for days, but never was he seen again.

Georgina (*putting a placating hand on his arm*) Poor Uncle!

Uncle (*shrugging it off*) 'Twas all me own fault. (*Crossing to the table down* R) I took to the devil drink and lost me job, me self-respect, me—everything. (*He sags over the table*)

Georgina But when my mother died—your distant relative—I came to care for you. (*Taking a pace forward*) Always rely on me!   HARRAH

A chord from the orchestra

Uncle Dear sweet child. (*Moving to her*) Then give me a copper for some gin.

Georgina I have it not.

Uncle If you love me—give me money!

Georgina But, uncle . . .

Uncle Give me money, woman, before I strike you! (*He raises his fist*)   MoooO

Georgina Stop! Stop! (*Aside*) What shall I do?

Uncle I must have gin. (*He grabs her by the throat and her head, facing out front, shakes from side to side on each of the next three words*) Gin! Gin! Gin!

Georgina sighs gracefully and, as Uncle releases her and turns to the rent tin on the table, she faints to the floor, having checked behind her first of all. (If the stage is low and the auditorium not raked, she can faint standing up)

(*Turning back from the table*) What's this? She's fainted! Now's me chance! (*He goes to the tin and takes some, but not all, of the money from it. This should raise a chorus of boos and hisses from the audience, so that his next words are addressed directly to them*) I'll not take it all. I have some decency left. Just tenpence. (*Making for the exit* L) The price of a bottle of gin!

Boos
Boos
Hisses

Boos.

Uncle exits, returns immediately for his cap, then goes again

Georgina (*awakening; quite matter-of-fact*) Where am I?

There is a long series of thunderous knocks off R
Georgina gets up, straightens her hair and dress, moving down L
The knocks stop

Come in.

The Landlord enters R, *standing just inside the entrance*

Landlord Ah-ha! (*He strides round the room looking in all directions. Having gone full circuit, he finishes up very close to Georgina*) All alone?
Georgina (*curtseying*) Yes, sir. My guardian has gone for—a walk.
Landlord And I've come for—the rent.
Georgina Yes, sir. (*Going to the tin*) I have it here.
Landlord (*furious*) Good. (*He moves* C)

Georgina hands him the tin. He rattles it

What's this? There's some missin', duckie.
Georgina That cannot be!
Landlord (*opening the tin with a flip of his wrist and looking inside*) Tenpence, to be precise.
Georgina Tenpence?
Landlord (*leering*) I want it!
Georgina It was all there a moment ago.
Landlord No excuses! (*Holding out his hand*) The residue!
Georgina Where can it be? (*Aside, moving* L) Uncle!

The Landlord puts the tin back on the table

Oh, no! And yet—a bottle of gin costs tenpence . . . Oh Uncle, how could you! What shall I do?
Landlord (*moving* C, *with a great swirl of his cape, and his eyes glittering with concupiscence*) Well—gel?
Georgina Oh sir, have pity! A simple miscalculation. Wait a few days and you shall have it all.
Landlord Impossible! The rent is due today, and today I mean to have it. If not—(*pointing* R)—out—(*He realises he is pointing the wrong way*)—out you go!   BOOS   HISSES
Georgina But where?
Landlord Into the streets, for all I care! (*He laughs cruelly*)
Georgina (*dropping to her knees and taking his hand*) Is there nothing I can do to soften your heart?
Landlord (*looking at her at his feet, then slowly looking at the audience*) Perhaps . . .
Georgina Please tell me what—I'll do anything!   Dirty Laugh
Landlord Anything . . . ?
Georgina Oh, yes.

Landlord (*behind his free hand*) Me luck's in! (*To her*) Then come here, me little wench—(*pulling her up*)—and let me put me arms around ye! (*He pulls her up so that she turns inwards towards him: he takes her by the waist and lowers her so that her head is facing R, the hand of her outstretched R arm on the floor supporting her body. He buries his face in her neck upstage of her face*)

Georgina Oh, no! Not that!

Landlord You said "anything".

Georgina But I am an innocent girl!

Landlord And I mean to have my tenpenny worth of you! (*He kisses her again*)

Georgina Oh no! Help! Help!

A handsome young man enters R

Man (*at the door*) Unhand that lady, you uncouth villain!

The Landlord releases Georgina and stands. Georgina, whose arm has been supporting her, is left rigid

Landlord What's that? (*He realizes Georgina is still there, turns and lifts her up, keeping his arm round her waist*) What business is it of yours, you young whippersnapper?

Man (*coming down the audience and explaining*) I heard a scream for help as I was passing in the street. (*Back to the action*) Now sir, whoever you are—let her go. (*He makes a grand gesture*)

Landlord (*producing a knife from his R trousers pocket*) Try and make me!

Georgina Oh, pray be careful, sir!

Man Don't worry, miss, I've dealt with scum like him before.

Landlord (*releasing Georgina and advancing*) Why, you . . .

The Landlord lunges very clumsily with his knife. The Man simply takes it between his thumb and finger and casually tosses it over his shoulder. The Landlord gazes stupified at his empty hand, then recovers and, with a snarl, raises his L fist. The Man carefully punches him on the nose, and the Landlord collapses on the floor.

Man That'll teach you to molest young girls.

Landlord (*grovelling*) Don't hit me again, sir, please! I didn't mean any harm. (*With a flash of his old venom*) But she owes me money!

Man (*out front*) Is this true?

Georgina (*out front*) Yes, sir. Tenpence for the rent.

Man (*taking a small money bag from his pocket*) Here, worm. (*He throws it on the floor*)

Landlord (*grabbing it*) Thank you, sir.

Man And now (*He raises his arm as though to strike the landlord*)

The Landlord cringes

—get out! (*And he merely gestures to the door*)

Landlord Of course, of course, sir. Thank you, sir. Right away, sir.

The Landlord exits practically on his knees, touching his forelock

Man Good riddance to bad rubbish, say I.

This should get cheers

The landlord returns and takes his bow, which should be very full and protracted, and then leaves again

And now, miss.

They turn to each other, gasp, and take a step back
(*Out front*) I love you. Will you marry me?

Georgina (*turning out front at the same time*) Yes!

They turn inwards and look at each other rapturously. They take a step back with their arms outstretched and then walk towards each other for a kiss. Just before they meet, Uncle is heard off L, *singing. They take a pace away from each other*

Man Botheration!

Uncle enters with a gin bottle, very drunk

Uncle (*singing as he enters*) "—where we used to sit and dream Nellie Dean", etc. (*He weaves about upstage, putting his cap on the stand*)

Man Who's this?

Georgina My guardian.

Man Drunk?

Georgina He's to be pitied. 'Tis tragedy has made him what he is.

Man I will respect him, then.

Uncle (*coming between them, and gazing drunkenly and closely at the Man*) Who are you? You're not Nellie. (*He crosses drunkenly to* L *of the Man*)

Man I, sir, am a millionaire.

Uncle (*matter-of-fact*) Millionaire. (*He takes a pace away then gives a double-take*) So young?

Man (*posing smiling at the audience on the words "so young"*) Yes, sir, as a result of a devilish clever invention of mine. (*He takes a pace forward*) The Safety Pin.

A chord of music. The Man takes a pace back

Uncle (*attempting to address the space just vacated*) You—(*realizing the Man is not there*)—you invented the shafety pin?

Man Yes, sir. And I have other inventions planned for making more millions. Me next is to be called—(*He takes a pace forward*)—the Zip Fastener!

A chord of music. The man steps back. Georgina blushes at this naughty word. Uncle repeats the business of addressing the empty space

Uncle What's—what's that?

Man (*taking Georgina's hand*) Give me permission to marry your ward, and you shall share me secrets.

The Man and Georgina gaze into each other's eyes

Uncle I give me consent. (*With a cry of self-pity, staggering down* L) But who'll look after me now? Alone again, this time—for ever. (*He drinks from his bottle*)

Georgina (*going to Uncle and putting her hand on his arm*) But Uncle, you'll always have me.

Uncle shrugs off her arm and raises the bottle to his lips

Man Stay, sir!

Uncle splutters

There is something familiar about your features (*Pronounced "fee-a-tures"*)

Uncle feels his face worriedly

Have we met before? (*He holds a pose with his L arm outstretched Uncle staggers across the stage, looks closely at the Man's hand, his arm, his L ear. The Man reacts from the drunken breath*

Uncle Not that I know of. (*He staggers behind the Man to R of him*) What's your name?

Man (*very big, with his hand on his brow despairingly*) Alas!

Uncle jumps with shock

I do not know. (*He takes up a position C for his big speech*) I was struck by a horse tram while crossing the street when but a child, and lost me memory as a result. (*Very big, indeed*) For the past fifteen years I have been searching for me—(*brokenly*)—identity.

Uncle does a double-take, then another, then a third which jumps him right off his feet

Uncle Fifteen years! Hic! Is it possible? *Hic!* Can it be? HIC! Are you—my—Roger?

Man (*something stirring*) Roger?

Uncle I lost me little boy fifteen years ago because of a momen-momen- momentary inattention. But how shall we ever know if you—(*Pointing*)—be—(*Pointing with the other hand*)—he? (*He gets his fingers all confused*)

Georgina (*very loudly*) The birthmark, Uncle!

Uncle nearly falls over with the shock. There is a chord of music

(*Moving LC*) You said that Roger had a heart-shaped mole upon his arm!

Man (*staggering back*) I have such a mark! (*He bares his L arm— nothing. He bares his R arm, and we see a large heart-shaped strawberry-coloured mark*)

Uncle rips the mark off—it is made of painted Elastoplast. The Man yells with pain

Uncle It's true. (*He slaps the birthmark over his heart*) Roger, my son!

Man Daddy!

They fall into each other's arms, with Uncle's face downstage

Uncle I thought you were dead. (*Moving to Georgina*)Instead, he's a millionaire! Away, bottle—(*He attempts to throw the gin bottle away, but his finger is stuck in the top*)—away—away, bottle—(*He manages to throw the bottle over his shoulder*)

The Man catches it and puts it on the table down R

—I've done with you. (*He passes Georgina over to the Man*) There's so much more to live for now!

Introductory music starts

All (*singing and dancing*)
> "Yield not to temptation
> For yielding is sin.
> Try drinking some water,
> It's much better than gin.
> Shun the doctrine of evil,
> Stay steadfast and true;
> Trust in the Almighty—
> He knows better than you!"

BLACK-OUT

The Music for "Yield Not To Temptation" will be found on page 38.

THE WAGES OF SIN
OR
PERFIDIOUS PIECEWORK

CHARACTERS

Lord Peregrine Fortune-Mint	A wronged husband
Jasper	A butler (?)
Mr Brown	Another wronged husband
Lady Priscilla Fortune-Mint	The wife
Mrs Brown	
The Chairman	

THE WAGES OF SIN
OR
PERFIDIOUS PIECEWORK

*There are entrances up L and up R. LC is a table covered with a cloth;
the legs of the table are covered with cloth of the same material,
except the downstage leg—the table should be angled to show this.
The cover for this leg is on the table. On the Chairman's table down
R is a Bible and a tray with a bottle of champagne and four champagne glasses—plastic sundae dishes will do very well.*

Chairman We come now to our dramatic interlude of high moral
and salutary intent, entitled *The Wages of Sin*!

The Tabs, if any, open. There is a chord of music

The setting, as is immediately apparent even to the most myopic,
is of course the exquisitely appointed drawing-room of Mint
Manor, the vast palatial country seat of the Fortune-Mints, one
of the oldest and noblest families of England. I must warn
those of a nervous disposition during this item to avert their
gaze or to take refuge beneath the seats and tables—who knows?
—the entertainment there may be far more interesting. To
continue, the dramatis personae consist of the following:

> Jasper the butler, who's first to appear;
> He's old and he's frail, so give him a cheer!

*Music, "John Brown's Body" played very slowly. Jasper enters
L. He bows very shakily, nearly falling over. The Chairman pushes
him upright, turns him, and points him to the exit R. Jasper totters
off R.*

> And here is the master, young Lord Mint;
> He's never known what it's like to be skint!

Music, "A Fine Old English Gentleman". Lord Mint enters R and bows graciously. If there are any boos he looks rather hurt and disconcerted—if somewhat vacuous—and exits L

> Now Lady Priscilla who leads the good life,
> Show respect for his lordship's trouble and strife!

Music "O Star of Eve" from "Tannhauser". Lady Priscilla sweeps on L, sweetly and decorously, curtseys to the audience, extends her hand for the Chairman to kiss, and exits R

The stage is set, the players are waiting in the wings, so now let us behold Mr Andrew Sachs's tragic disaster *The Wages of Sin!* or—*Perfidious Piecework!*

The lights Black-out. Dramatic music is heard, which fades as the lights came up again.

Lord Fortune-Mint enters. He strolls over-nonchalantly from L to RC, glances at the table LC,.blanches, and calls

Lord Fortune-Mint Jasper! Jasper!

Jasper enters R, very tottery and shaky

Jasper Yes, my lord?
Lord Fortune-Mint (*with his L hand shielding his face*) Jasper, the leg of that table is—is—uncovered!

Jasper turns, and falls backward with horror into Lord Fortune-Mint's arms

Jasper Ooooh! Most distressing, my lord. It's the chambermaid, sir. She's so forgetful.
Lord Fortune-Mint Where is she?
Jasper Who, my lord?
Lord Fortune-Mint The chambermaid. Where is the chamber-maid?
Jasper I don't know, my lord, but the teapot was made in Staffordshire.
Lord Fortune-Mint (*impatiently*) Cover up that—leg, Jasper. At once!
Jasper Yes, my lord. (*He totters over to the table LC, lowers himself to his knees, and places the cover over the leg*)

Lord Fortune-Mint Suppose Lady Priscilla, my pure angelic wife to whom I, Lord Peregrine Fortune-Mint, have been devotedly married these past ten years and who is sole heir to my vast estates and fortunes, should witness this—debauchery! That perverted servant! Turn her out of Mint Manor this very day!

Jasper (*rising to his feet*) Very good, my lord. (*He takes a step or two to the exit* R, *then reacts*) Ah! Here *is* Lady Priscilla—(*He takes a big breath*)—your pure angelic wife to whom you, Lord Peregrine Fortune-Mint have been devotedly married these past ten years and who is sole heir to your vast estates and fortunes—(*He takes a breath*)—now, my lord!

Lord Fortune-Mint (*sweeping down* L) Priscilla, my darling!

Music. Lady Priscilla sweeps on in a long black cloak. Jasper bows up LC *and starts to topple forward*

Lady Priscilla Peregr—(*She pushes Jasper upright and resumes her welcoming smile*) Peregrine! (*She goes to Lord Fortune-Mint*)

They embrace fondly but chastely

Lord Fortune-Mint Are you riding again this morning, my heart-blossom?

Lady Priscilla (*moving to the Chairman's table down* R) No, no, Peregrine, don't you remember? (*She sits on the Chairman's chair*) Today I leave to do some more of my Good Works among the backward natives across the Channel.

Lord Fortune-Mint Oh yes, of course. (*Moving* C) Take care of yourself, my only treasure. You are unique.

Lady Priscilla Not so, my love.

Lord Fortune-Mint Not so? How so, not so?

Lady Priscilla I have a twin sister.

Lord Fortune-Mint A twin sister? How amusing. (*Giving a gay laugh to underline the point*) Ten years married and I did not know.

Lady Priscilla It must have slipped my mind. Yes, we are as alike as two—(*Rather embarrassed at having to say a slightly naughty word*)—peas. Even Mama could not tell us apart.

Lord Fortune-Mint (*going down on one knee by her side*) She cannot be as lovely as you. (*He looks out front*)

Lady Priscilla Perhaps not. (*She rises and goes round the chair to above it, picking up the Bible from the table*)

Lord Fortune-Mint (*not noticing that she has gone*) I already have everything I want. (*He turns and leans in for a kiss, crashing down onto the chair*)

Lady Priscilla (*moving* C) Now I must leave.

Lord Fortune-Mint (*rising, speaking out front*) Good-bye Priscilla.

Lady Priscilla I shall be gone some weeks.

Lord Fortune-Mint (*out front*) How shall I live without you?

Lady Priscilla (*indicating the Bible*) We all must do our duty.

Lord Fortune-Mint (*dropping his head*) I understand.

Music plays "Amen"

Jasper (*moving down to the audience*) How brave and admirable.

(*He gets the audience to applaud, then totters back up* LC)

Lady Priscilla (*up* C) Good-bye, Jasper.

Jasper (*tearfully*) Good-bye, my lady. (*He bows*)

Lady Priscilla pushes him upright

Lady Priscilla And now I go—to catch a packet!

Lady Priscilla sweeps off R, *followed by a weeping Jasper*

Lord Fortune-Mint (*giving one rather phoney sob*) Alone again for several weeks. (*He gives another sob, walks to the table* LC, *sobs again*) I cannot bear these partings from my dear wife. (*He leans on the table in despair, then notices the table-legs. A prurient gleam comes into his eyes: he glances round to see that the coast is clear, then drops to his knees, lifts the downstage table-leg cover, and fondles the leg lasciviously, giggling and slavering*)

Jasper enters, sees what is going on, and reacts with shock and horror. Then he coughs.

Lord Fortune-Mint straightens up hurriedly, banging his head on the underneath of the table in the process

Lord Fortune-Mint (*ultra-calmly*) What is it, Jasper?

Jasper My lord, Lady Priscilla, your dear wife, is now safely aboard the steam packet, for Calais and has left the shores of England.

Lord Fortune-Mint (*suffering nobly*) Thank you, Jasper. (*He wanders down* L)

Jasper There is also someone to see you, my lord.

Lord Fortune-Mint Not now, Jasper.

Jasper (*crossing* R) This is a lady, my lord, who bears a striking resemblance to her ladyship. I doubt if even Lady Priscilla's mama could tell them apart.

Lord Fortune-Mint A lady who resembles my wife? Who can it be? (*He gives a start*) Ah! (*Putting one hand on his brow*) Is it possible?

Jasper What, my lord?

Lord Fortune-Mint Could it be my wife's—twin sister?

Jasper (*Also with one hand on his brow*) Ah! There is one thing that makes me doubt that, my lord.

Lord Fortune-Mint What, Jasper, what?

Jasper It's true that facially they are as alike as two—peas—

Both their heads drop embarrassedly for a second

—but in the matter of deportment and manner . . .

Lord Fortune-Mint Deportment and manner?

Jasper Well, my lord, her ladyship is pure, angelic and modest, but this lady—(*He chuckles naughtily, shaking a leg suggestively*) —she's—well, she's . . .

Lord Fortune-Mint (*moving* C) Show her in, Jasper! (*Changing his enthusiastic tone when he sees he is giving his basically concupiscent nature away*) We cannot turn our backs on the less fortunate among us. Show her in.

Jasper (*still chuckling obscenely*) Very, good, my lord.

Jasper exits R

Lord Fortune-Mint Priscilla in France, and a sister who is impure, immodest and in-angelic, eh?

Jasper enters R

Jasper This way, madam.

Lord Fortune-Mint moves down L

Mrs Brown! (*He stands up* LC)

Slow Blues music. The lights lower, and a white arm appears from behind the wing, to be followed by the voluptuous Mrs Brown, in a very fetching decolleté dress. She sinks into a provocative curtsey as the music finishes and the lights come up. Her following-spot changes back from red to pink.

Mrs Brown Lord Fortune-Mint!
Lord Fortune-Mint You—(*his voice cracks*)—you are my wife's twin sister!
Mrs Brown (*rising and taking a pace back*) You've guessed!

Jasper moves to middle C and follows the following exchange with rapid movements of the head like a tennis spectator

Lord Fortune-Mint Her identical twin!
Mrs Brown You knew!
Lord Fortune-Mint Am I right?
Mrs Brown Yes!

Jasper begins to topple backwards with amazement

Lord Fortune-Mint Jasper!
Jasper (*pulling himself together with a great effort*) Yes, my lord?
Lord Fortune-Mint Champagne!
Jasper Yes, my lord.

Lord Fortune-Mint moves towards Mrs Brown as Jasper moves to the table down R. There is a slight collision as Jasper gets between the other two. Jasper picks up the tray and turns

Lord Fortune-Mint You are as beautiful as my wife . . .
Mrs Brown No more?

Lord Fortune-Mint takes her hand to kiss it as Jasper ploughs between them bearing the tray. Mrs Brown's glove comes off in Lord Fortune-Mint's hand and she turns upstage a pace or two. Lord Fortune-Mint does not notice and tries to kiss the empty glove. He reacts and turns, putting the glove in his pocket. Jasper meanwhile puts the champagne tray on the table LC. Mrs Brown sits on the chair down R

Lord Fortune-Mint You may go now, Jasper. (*He moves C and picks up the champagne bottle*)

Jasper exits R, *pausing only to shake a leg and chortle at Mrs Brown*

Mrs Brown puts her reticule on the table down R. *Lord Fortune-Mint attempts to open the champagne bottle, holding it between his legs in what can only be described as an unfortunately suggestive position*

This is a noble vintage! (*After a great struggle the cork drops out and falls dully to the floor.* PRODUCER'S NOTE: *this is a big laugh and does not need an accompanying "pop" noise effect off-stage*) Why have you come? (*He mimes pouring champagne into two glasses*)

Mrs Brown Because I'm—lonely.

Lord Fortune-Mint (*standing with the champagne glasses*) Your sister is not—(*taking one pace to her*)—here.

Mrs Brown Then we are—(*Rising and taking a glass*)—alone? Just you and —(*she drinks*)—I?

Lord Fortune-Mint (*drinking hastily*) Yes.

Mrs Brown May she return—(*She drinks*)—unexpectedly?

Lord Fortune-Mint No, she's gone a—(*He drinks*)—broad. (*Bitterly*) Ten years we have been married and for five of them she's been abroad to do Good Works. (*He drinks*)

Mrs Brown (*with a light laugh, crossing below him to down* L) You poor unhappy man!

Lord Fortune-Mint (*getting a grip on himself temporarily*) Ah, no! She is my one true love, and I am faithful unto death. (*Moving to her*) But you are so much more exciting than dull, virtuous Priscilla. (*He pulls her by her* R *arm to face him*) I can't resist you!

Mrs Brown (*after a beat pause*) Kiss me!

They both hurl their champagne glasses aside. Lord Fortune-Mint takes her in a sweeping embrace so that her head is pointing to the entrance up R

Jasper enters, reacts violently at what he sees, then recovers himself

Jasper My lord, My lord!

They are oblivious

Mrs Brown's husband is here! Lord Fortune-Mint! It's Mr Brown

Mr Brown crashes on to suitable music, sweeping Jasper to R of the entrance

Mr Brown Villain (*Out front*) Unhand that woman!

Chord of music

Mrs Brown (*still in Lord Fortune-Mint's embrace, with her head upside down*) Algernon!

Chord of music

Lord Fortune-Mint (*lifting Mrs Brown up*) What is the meaning of this?

Mr Brown (*taking a pace forward and speaking out front*) I am her—husband!

Lord Fortune-Mint Her husband! (*To Mrs Brown*) Then—who are you?

Mrs Brown I am—his wife!

Lord Fortune-Mint His wife!

Mrs Brown Yes—we are married! To each other!

Lord Fortune-Mint Married to each other! Of course! You were announced as *Mrs* Brown! You cunning fiend—I should have guessed you had a husband.

Mr Brown (*producing a pistol*) Your last moment has come, sir!

Lord Fortune-Mint Jasper—throw him out!

Jasper Yes, my lord. (*He makes for Mr Brown with a "rolling-up-sleeve" mime*)

Mr Brown backs until they are both parallel with the exit up R. Mr Brown then takes a deep breath and blows

Jasper falls out of sight

Mr Brown Defend yourself, wife stealer! (*He moves back C, and throws another pistol to Lord Fortune-Mint*)

Mrs Brown (*running across to R of Mr Brown*) Oh, stop! Stop! I cannot bear the sound of shots!

Mr Brown Don't worry, my dear—there'll only be one. His gun isn't loaded. (*He laughs*)

Mrs Brown No, no, not even one shot, I pray you.

Lord Fortune-Mint If you were a gentleman, sir, you'd respect the lady's wishes.

Mr Brown Very well—on guard. (*He takes up a fencing position*)

Lord Fortune-Mint does the same, and they fence back and forth with the pistols, to "hurry music". Eventually Mr Brown is stabbed and falls, writhing horribly in his death throes. In the process he pulls off the upstage table-leg cover. He holds it aloft for a moment, then collapses dead. Lord Fortune-Mint drops his gun in horror

Mrs Brown Ah, my poor husband! (*Bending over Mr Brown*) Killer! Assassin! Murdered! All life gone! A shattered corpse! An empty shell! A stiff! (*She weeps*)

Lord Fortune-Mint You don't mean . . .

Mrs Brown Yes—dead! You brutal ruffian! (*Making for the exit up* R) Oh, my husband! My lover! My life! I shall throw myself in the moat!

Mrs Brown exits but returns immediately

You do have a moat?

Lord Fortune-Mint (*matter-of-fact*) I'm afraid not.

Mrs Brown Oh!

Her face creases into further tears and she exits again

Lord Fortune-Mint (*moving* C) What shall I do? (*He looks at his arm and reacts violently*) I'm wounded! Just a scraze. (*He takes Mrs Brown's glove from his pocket*) This will staunch the flow. (*He winds it round his arm and moves down* R)

Jasper enters up R

Jasper My lord, my lord! Lady Priscilla, your pure and angelic wife, has returned unexpectedly from abroad and is coming in the house now, my lord!

Lord Fortune-Mint What! She mustn't see the bloody corpse. Get rid of it, Jasper.

Jasper Yes, my lord. (*He bends down and "lifts" the corpse on to his back, so that they are both facing the same way, with Mr Brown's arms over Jasper's shoulders*)

Jasper turns so that he and the corpse are both facing the exit up R

   Lady Priscilla sweeps on up R

Lady Priscilla Darling Peregrine, I have returned unexpectedly
   from . . . (*She sees Jasper and the corpse*) Ah! What does this
   mean? It is Mr Brown! The husband of my twin sister and
   therefore my brother-in-law! (*She lifts the corpse's head*) Dead!
   (*She let's the head drop back on Jasper's L shoulder*) That will be
   all, Jasper.
Jasper Yes, my lady.

   Jasper and the corpse shuffle off up R

Lady Priscilla Now, Peregrine. What have you been up to in my
   absence? You stand there with a guilty expression on your face,
   a lady's glove on your arm, an open bottle of champagne on the
   table, two glasses and two guns on the floor. (*She picks up
   Mr Brown's gun*)

   *Mr Brown enters and takes a lengthy call. Lady Priscilla and
   Lord Fortune-Mint hold out their upstage hands to him. Mr Brown
   exits*

   I see it all. While I have been abroad doing Good Works you
   have been unfaithful to me with my own twin sister. (*She moves
   C*)

*Lord Fortune-Mint also moves C, vainly trying to interrupt during
the rest of her speech*

   Her husband found you—drunk—together; you fought and
   callously you murdered him, thinking to keep your shameless
   behaviour a secret from me and from society. Is this true?
Lord Fortune-Mint (*matter-of-fact*) Yes, it's true.
Lady Priscilla My husband an adulterous murderer!
Lord Fortune-Mint There is only one honourable course left to
   me now.
Lady Priscilla You don't mean—oh, no! (*But she holds the gun
   out to him*)
Lord Fortune-Mint I'm sorry, Priscilla.

Lady Priscilla (*moving down* L; *charitably*) I forgive you, Peregrine.
Lord Fortune-Mint Good-bye, Priscilla.
Lady Priscilla Good-bye, Peregrine.

Lord Fortune-Mint points the gun at his heart and pulls the trigger. Silence. He glances nervously towards the wings, and pulls the trigger again. Again there is silence. Angrily he turns upstage and makes for the exit up R *to see what is delaying the gunshot: after he has taken two steps the shot is fired. Lord Fortune-Mint staggers back downstage with his back to the audience, during which time he is fixing a very phoney-looking bloodstain to his waistcoat. ("Velcro" is very good for this effect.) When it is attached, he turns round gesturing wildly to his wound so that we all see it clearly. He staggers round in desperate death-throes and falls, pulling off the* L *table-leg cover: he holds it aloft for an instant, then collapses, dead*

Lady Priscilla Jasper!

Jasper enters

Jasper Yes, my lady?

Lord Fortune-Mint rises, takes his call, and lies down again

Lady Priscilla Observe! (*She indicates the corpse*)

Jasper reacts violently, then rapidly peels off his wig and whiskers

Jasper At last! We're free!

They embrace C. *A chord of music*

And all his money to which you are sole heir is ours!
Lady Priscilla Yes, but no one will ever know the full truth.
Jasper You mean that it was all a cleverly contrived plot on our part.
Lady Priscilla Yes! Only you and I know that I have no twin sister! That I am also—Mrs Brown!

Music. Lady Priscilla removes her cloak and goes to the table down R, *placing the cloak on the chair*

Poor Peregrine! (*She laughs*) When he thought I was doing Good Works abroad, I was in reality being the devoted wife of the even wealthier Mr Brown, who has also made me his sole heir!

Jasper (*moving* C *and pouring champange into the other two glasses on the table* LC) Don't forget that I'm entitled to half of everything for helping you.

Lady Priscilla You, Jasper? No, you fool! You've outlived your usefulness and know too much! (*She fires once: there is a sound effect off-stage and one champagne glass flies into the air; she fires again and the other glass goes flying; the third shot strikes Jasper*)

Jasper clutches himself. His death should be especially spectacular, Eventually he falls, ripping off the R *table-leg cover. He holds it aloft then collapses motionless. An instant later, he shakes his leg in a final spasm. Then he rises and takes a bow, after which he resumes his position*

They say the Wages of Sin is Death, but I've proved them wrong! (*She laughs*) The Wages of Sin is pleasure! Yes, pleasure, I tell you! Pleasure, luxury and lust! (*Moving* C) There's nothing in my way, now . . . (*She is struck by a pain*)

The music changes to mysterioso. The lights dim

What is this fearful pain? Ah yes—it is my old condition. The consequence of too much abandoned dissipation—ah!—it is creeping up my legs—this is more serious than I thought. My pills! My pills! (*She struggles to the table down* R *and takes a pill-box from her reticule. She opens the box and swallows a pill. Immediately she clutches her throat in agony, and looks at the label on the pill-box*) Ah, poison (*Taking another pill-box from the reticule*) The wrong pill-box! This is poison intended for Jasper and my husbands had my plot misfired . . . Oh, I repent my evil ways, I swear I do. (*With a ray of hope*) Ah, yes, I remember now the antidote to this deadly poison is champagne! (*She puts the pill-boxes down, picks up a gun, and lurches over to the table* LC. *There she manages to pick up the champagne bottle and take a swig. We see her face change from agony to triumph*)

The lights come up to full

Saved! And now it's back to the devil, the world and the flesh! (*She drinks again and moves* C) The Grim Reaper is foiled again! (*Moving to the table down* R) No, I'll not be reaped yet awhile. Life is to be enjoyed—(*She drinks*)—to the dregs! (*She puts the bottle on the table down* R) Life is to be lived! (*She points the gun wildly to the ceiling and fires a shot. She clasps herself*) Ah! I am shot. (*She staggers* C) The bullet hit the crystal chandelier and ricocheted into my breast! (*She rails at her fate*)

The lights begin to lower

Is Death to claim me at last? (*She weeps*) No, no! I am too young to die. (*She kneels. With resignation*) So, now—retribution. (*She pulls herself slowly to her feet*) Take heed, all you evil doers—there is no escape. (*Clutching the table* LC) Repent your evil ways—the Wages of Sin *is* Deeeeath! (*She grabs the downstage table-leg cover which comes off and wraps itself round her throat. She chokes and dies*)

BLACK-OUT

CURTAIN

Music for call: March in C from *Tannhauser*

YIELD NOT TO TEMPTATION

Yield not to temp-ta - tion, for yield-ing is sin, try drink-ing some wat - er, it's much bet-ter than gin; shun the doc-trine of e - vil, stay stead-fast and true; trust in the al - might - ty, he knows bet-ter than you!

FURNITURE AND PROPERTY LIST

Furniture and property list
On stage throughout all three plays: Chairman's table and chair (*down R*)

MARIA MARTEN

On stage: Nil

Off stage: (R) Sign with "Maria's Kitchen" on one side and "The Old
Red Barn" on the other (**Stage Manager**)
(R) Shovel (to be handed to **Corder**)
(R) Napstick (for gun-shot)

Personal: **Maria:** note in stocking
Corder: gun in pocket

THE DRUNKARD'S DILEMMA

On stage: *On Chairman's table:* flip-top tin marked "RENT" containing
half a dozen pennies

Off stage: (R) Hat-stand (to be handed to **Chairman**)
(L) Gin bottle (**Uncle**)

Personal: **Georgina:** shawl
ten pennies
Landlord: knife
Man: grouch bag containing coins
birthmark on R arm (shirt sleeves not to be fastened)

THE WAGES OF SIN

On stage: Table (LC), covered with cloth and with three of the legs
covered with the same material. These covers must come off
easily, and can simply be secured by a piece of elastic tied
round the top of the leg. A fourth leg cover is set on the
table: this cover should be slightly weighted to facilitate
Lady Priscilla's inadvertent self-strangulation. The table is
slightly angled to the floats

On Chairman's table: Bible. Tray with bottle of champagne and four glasses (plastic); the bottle is empty, and the cork needs to be cut down and reinserted. The wire and foil can be replaced for easy removal. The plastic glasses break easily, and spares should be readily available.

Off stage: (R) Napstick for gunshots. This is simply, two long pieces of wood hinged together. The shots can be worked by **Mr Brown**

Personal: **Lady Priscilla:** reticule containing 2 pill-boxes
Mr Brown: 2 small pistols
Lord Fortune-Mint: bloodstain ("Velcro")

LIGHTING PLOT

Property fittings required: nil

In addition to the general lighting, suitably coloured following-spots should be used for the various characters

MARIA MARTEN

A kitchen; a barn

To open:	General lighting	
Cue 1	**Corder** enters *Lights flash off and on*	(Page 4)
Cue 2	**Corder:** ". . . in the Old Red Barn" *Lights flash off and on*	(Page 5)
Cue 3	**Corder:** ". . . you sealed your doom" *Lights flash off and on*	(Page 6)
Cue 4	**Stage-Manager** exits *Lights lower*	(Page 6)
Cue 5	**Maria** enters *Lights up to full*	(Page 7)
Cue 6	**Maria** dies *Lights lower*	(Page 9)
Cue 7	**Corder** exits *Black-out, then up to full for Calls*	(Page 9)

THE DRUNKARD'S DILEMMA

A humble living-room

To open:	General lighting	
Cue 1	ALL: ". . . better than you!" *Black-out, then up to full for Calls*	(Page 22)

THE WAGES OF SIN

A palatial room

To open:	General lighting	
Cue 1	**Chairman:** ". . . Perfidious Piecework" *Black-out, then up to full*	(Page 26)
Cue 2	**Jasper:** "Mrs Brown" *Lights lower*	(Page 29)
Cue 3	As **Mrs Brown** curtseys *Lights up to full*	(Page 30)
Cue 4	**Lady Priscilla** is struck by a pain *Lights lower*	(Page 36)
Cue 5	**Lady Priscilla** drinks champagne *Lights up to full*	(Page 36)
Cue 6	**Lady Priscilla:** ". . . into my breast" *Lights lower*	(Page 37)
Cue 7	**Lady Priscilla** dies *Black-out, then up to full for Calls*	(Page 37)

EFFECTS PLOT

MARIA MARTEN

Cue 1	**Corder:** ". . . tripping across the fields" *Heavy footsteps* R	(Page 7)
Cue 2	**Corder** takes two steps to R exit *Gunshot*	(Page 8)

THE DRUNKARD'S DILEMMA

No cues

THE WAGES OF SIN

Cue 1	**Lord Fortune-Mint** goes to exit up R *Gunshot*	(Page 35)
Cue 2	**Lady Priscilla** fires pistol 3 times *Three gunshots*	(Page 36)
Cue 3	**Lady Priscilla** fires at ceiling *Gunshot*	(Page 37)

MARIA MARTEN

Costumes

Maria: Simple three-quarter length gingham dress with apron.

Corder: Morning coat and striped trousers, with fancy waistcoat and cravat. Top-hat and cloak.

Stage Manager: Collar-less shirt with red choker, boots, bowler hat, nondescript waistcoat and baggy trousers.

Make-up

Maria: Straight—not too healthy and robust.

Corder: Heavy eyebrows, dark-brown line under the eyes, green eyeshadow. Curly moustache.

Stage Manager: Unshaven, red nose—not too exaggerated.

THE DRUNKARD'S DILEMMA

COSTUMES

Georgina: Simple dress, or blouse and skirt (light-coloured). Shawl.

Uncle: Collar-less shirt, muffler, boots, corduroy trousers and non-matching scruffy jacket. Cap.

Landlord: Morning Suit with cloak and top-hat. Gloves.

Man: White trousers and striped blazer. Boater.

MAKE-UP

Uncle: Unshaven, bushy eyebrows, lake under the eyes. For second entrance the nose can be reddened. Straggly moustache.

Georgina: Straight—pale and interesting.

Landlord: Robust-looking (Base: Leichner 5 and 4) Black moustache and heavy black eyebrows with dark brown under the eyes and white inside the lower eye-lids.

Man: Cleanshaven. Straight juvenile (Base: Leichner 5 and 9)

THE WAGES OF SIN

COSTUMES

Lord Fortune-Mint: Tweed plus-fours or period morning suit.

Jasper: Butler costume—rather too large. Wing collar, black tie.

Mr Brown: Any smart period suit. If played by the chairman, simply add a top hat and cloak. If a top hat is worn, the actor must be careful to get hold of it and take it off when he dies or when he takes his call.

Lady Priscilla: An all-enveloping black cloak.

Mrs Brown: A scarlet, very low cut evening dress, full length evening-gloves. Feathers in the hair and lots of sparklers. Perhaps also a boa.

MAKE-UP

Lady Priscilla ⎫
Mrs Brown   ⎬ As glamorous as possible.

Jasper: Straight (Leichner 5 and 4) under a white or
                               grey wig and matching moustache. The
                               moustache should not obscure the mouth or
                               much expression will be lost.

Lord Fortune-Mint: Straight (Leichner 5 and 4) with perhaps rather
                               supercilious eyebrows.

Mr Brown: Straight (Leichner 5 and 9) with perhaps a
                               small painted moustache. A painted-on
                               monocle is quite fun.